*How
Not
to
Write*

Other Books
by William Safire

How
Not
to
Write

THE
ESSENTIAL
MISRULES
OF
GRAMMAR

William
Safire

W · W · Norton & Company
New York   London

Manufacturing by The Maple-Vail Book Manufacturing Group
Book design by Margaret M. Wagner
Production manager: Amanda Morrison

For information about permission to reproduce selections from
this book, write to Permissions, W. W. Norton & Company, Inc.,
500 Fifth Avenue, New York, NY 10110

ISBN 0-393-32723-X

W. W. Norton & Company, Inc.
500 Fifth Avenue, New York, N.Y. 10110
www.wwwnorton.com

W. W. Norton & Company Ltd.
Castle House, 75-76 Wells Street, London W1T 3QT

2 3 4 5 6 7 8 9 0

*How
Not
to
Write*

Intro

*W*hat kind of word is *intro* for the beginning of a book laying down rules of grammar and usage? It's a clipped word, slang, a breezy informality entirely inappropriate to the job at hand.

Intro, let's face it, is a mistake in this highly literate context. *Introduction*—with its Latin meaning of "to lead within"—would be not only correct, but also more apt, considering the double meaning of *lead*. Better still would be *prolegomenon*, pronounced pro-le-GOM-en-on, which smacks of pedantry but would at least stop readers who automatically skip introductions.

But the sassy *intro* at the head of this non-sassy preface illustrates the essence of a fumblerule: a mistake that calls attention to the rule. The message: See how wrong this looks? Do as I say, not as I do.

We smile at the fumblerule's mistake and tell ourselves we're pretty smart not to do that dumb thing. With that boost to our grammatical self-esteem, we are prepared to swallow a little pedagogy. Not that any of us need it; we're all native speakers and don't need grammarians to tell us how to use our own language; still, we're made ready, by this device, to buy a bit of explanation.

Schoolteachers have been compiling lists of fumblerules for generations, posting them on bulletin boards and mailing them around. I ran a *New York Times Magazine* column listing some a few years ago and received scores more in the mail. Culled, winnowed, beefed up and edited, here are the best: a ferocious farrago of instructive error, each with an accompanying explanation, designed to straighten you out without weighing you down.

The most graphic fumblerule of all can be found tacked on office and school walls throughout the English-speaking world: "Plan Ahead," it says, with the last letters squeezed together, and the final *d* almost crowded off the page. That's the idea behind *How Not to Write*. Now let's apply it to the way we write and speak.

1

No sentence fragments.

*W*hat happens when you use a word that is not a verb, or write a phrase that does not contain a verb, as if it were a complete sentence? You see lying dangerously on the page a shard of prose called a *sentence fragment.*

Fragmentation occurs when an end mark of punctuation (period, question mark, exclamation point) follows an incomplete sentence.

As grammarians say, if you ain't got a verb, you ain't got a sentence. (Permissive grammarians.) To be a sentence, a run of words must be a complete thought, with a subject and a predicate—in other words, it must be about something or somebody taking action or being something.

Take the parenthetical words two sentences back, "Permissive grammarians"; the phrase should not be followed by a period because the thought is not complete. If I wanted to add an afterthought, I should have written, "(Permissive grammarians say that, to show their familiarity with dialect.)" The verb "say" makes it a sentence.

Not all sentence fragments are to be avoided. Why not? Because of their rhetorical effect. (The last two non-sentences are fragments that make my point. Is this a good pedagogical technique? Not always.)

A one-word sentence is possible only if the word is a verb in the imperative mood, with the subject clearly implied. Consider the Army sergeant who wishes to convey this message: "Because of the screaming sound you all hear of an incoming smart bomb, it behooves us all to evacuate this area." Instead, he will holler: *"Run!"* Although military purists will argue that he should shout *"Cover!"*, his grammar is correct.

Enough of this page. (Fragment.) *Turn!* (Complete sentence.)

2

Avoid run-on sentences they are hard to read.

A run-on, as every banker knows, is any incorrect joining of sentences.

One wrong method is *fusion,* the simple jamming together of two complete, stand-alone thoughts, as in our fumblerule. William Faulkner and James Joyce did that a lot and got away with it you are not them I am not them either.

A trickier wrong method is the *comma splice,* which joins two separate sentences with a comma that is just not up to the job. Don't do that, try something else. (Aha! That was a comma splice; see how awkwardly it slaps together the two thoughts?)

Here are three right ways to connect sentences:

1. Separate the main clauses with a semicolon, a form of punctuation that makes a full stop but continues to dribble. Note the artistic, stylish double sentence in the above paragraph, after the "Aha!"—the use of the semicolon avoids the choppiness of two short sentences, but seems to bring the second thought closer to the first, as if the two ideas were inseparable. (Never use a dash when a semicolon is called for, as I just did after the second "Aha!")

2. Use a conjunction, or as Kissingerians used to say, employ linkage. *And, or* and *but* coordinate separate thoughts evenhandedly, while *as, because, if, when, though* gently subordinate the clause that follows.

3. I lied; there are only two ways to connect sentences, and I used them both in this sentence.

Happily, a third choice is available to you: Do not connect two independent thoughts at all. Nowhere is it written that sentences require more than one complete thought.

Instead of linking, decouple. Use a period. Be choppy. Sometimes that's a strong way to write. Just don't do it too often or for too long. It makes the reader think you think he's a dope.

3

A writer must not
shift your
point of view.

*T*o some spokespersons, *person* is a combining form self-consciously used to achieve sexlessness. To grammarians, *person* is a glorious word to express an idea that helps organize the universe.

Person identifies the one who is speaking. That's *me* (or that is *I,* as the pedants say); *I* am doing the talking here, even when I use the royal or editorial *we,* and I am called *the first person.*

Person also separates the speaker from the one being spoken to (that's *you,* the reader or audience, called *the second person*); it's not a putdown, but somebody has to be first, and long ago it was decided that it was better me than you.

Finally, person separates me and you from those being spoken about (that's *them*—*he* and *she,* also taken together as *they*—as the subject). They are in *the third person.*

This rule may be hard for upwardly mobile people to swallow, but here it is: Stay in your place. It's not unfair; I have to stay in my place, and they have to stay in theirs. You cannot say, "They have to stay in your place" (unless you want a *ménage à trois*) any more than I can say, "I have to stay in their place." Stick to your person.

In the same way, be consistent about your point of view. As a writer, you are allowed to play God—to be omniscient (from *omni,* "all," and *scientia,* "knowledge," meaning "all-knowing").

4

Do not put statements
in the negative form.

In this know-it-all mode, you may write, "The frog thought the princess was cute; the princess thought the frog was ugly." But the reader doesn't really identify with either. That's why some writers write from the point of view of the frog ("He thought the princess was cute and assumed she thought the same of him"). That's consistent; describe what the princess does as it seems to the frog ("But then, when asked for a kiss, she went, 'Phooey!' and, to the frog's consternation, stormed out").

If you have chosen a frog's point of view, do not suddenly leap over to the mind of the princess. Stick to your person, stay in your place and you will discover how a frog of a writer, kissed by consistency, can become a prince.

*A*ssert yourself. Be positive. Strengthen your prose by admitting no doubt.

Now flip that paragraph: Don't hide your light under a bushel; don't be negative; never weaken your prose by admitting doubt.

See the difference? The first paragraph jacks you up and twists a knuckle in your spine, the way your mother or your sergeant used to; the second whines at you, reminds you of your wheedling brother-in-law— nag, nag, nag.

Not is a non-starter. "She was not what you would call neat" is better expressed as "She was a slob." Queen Victoria could get away with "We are not amused," but most of us today would do better with "We are bored stiff."

Same idea with *un-* and *non-* words; the hard hitters in the writing dodge avoid them when a positive word is available. For *untrustworthy,* use *false, deceitful, conniving* or whatever you mean; for *non-smoker,* say *sensible person.* (*Non-starter,* on the other hand, which comes from British racing slang for a scratched horse, is a lively word; use it freely.)

Remember this: Whenever you use an *un-,* you are signaling, "I don't know exactly what it is, but I sure know what it's not." It's like the amnesiac in Fred Allen's Alley, in the heyday of radio, who went around saying, "Who am I? I don't carry an umbrella, so I can't be Neville Chamberlain."

Note that I wrote *Remember this* and not *Don't forget this.* That's a speechwriter's trick. Whenever a speaker wants to cozy up to an audience, he urges them warmly to remember; when he wants to waggle his finger and annoy his audience, as some hellfire preachers and losing politicians do, he warns them sternly not to forget. The positive style persuades; the negative style turns off.

Above all, don't embrace ambiguity. (Now and then, for variety, it's effective to indulge in a negative.) But don't overdo it. (See? Nag, nag . . .)

5

*Don't use contractions
in formal writing.*

*I*f you're eager to shake hands with your reader, or there's some reason you won't be bothered by the difference between written and spoken English—or if you've discovered that writing in the formal style ain't easy—feel free to lollygag around with *won't, don't, doesn't, I'm, she'll* and the other manifestations of the easygoing style.

What Godfather of grammar, then, in this laid-back day and age, would dare to put out a contract on contractions?

You don't wear a tie to a ballgame, and you do not wear loafers to a church wedding. In the same way, you shouldn't use formal English when your intent is to be sassy or breezy, nor should you employ contractions in a solemn speech or formal letter.

This book is written in a studiously informal style in a frantic effort to help the medicine go down. I'll do linguistic nip-ups, crack wise and prestidigitate mightily to slip in a little painless pedagogy.

But if called upon to draft an Inaugural address, I'd elevate my style: I would stiffen my sinews as well as my prose, sweep away the slang, lengthen and slow my cadence, eschew all appealingly childlike mannerisms and call up the majesty and sonority of Standard English usage.

That means ixnay on contractions. You can't have it both ways: Either relax and contractionate around, or straighten up and write right.

Here's a reason, if in doubt, to lean toward the formal: *not* is a strong word. *I won't* sounds stubborn, but *I will not* sounds determined and slightly more emphatic. *I shall not,* spoken to a large audience, really digs those heels in.

To get across high purpose, let's use *Let us.* If the occasion calls for a jacket and tie, forgo contractions.

6

*The adverb always
follows the verb.*

*Y*ou will quickly see how eager copy editors are to push the adverb beyond the verb. (Keep your cotton-pickin' fingers away from that *quickly*; if I preferred *see quickly,* I would have decisively written it that way.)

Is there really much difference between *foolishly edit* and *edit foolishly?* No, not much—but occasionally, a nuance can be winkled out.

For example, you can say either *I talked to him regularly* or *I regularly talked to him,* but you cannot say *I severely talked to him* when you mean *I talked to him severely.* Some adverbs fortunately fit in front of a verb; others fall behind, luckily.

When you admonish your children on their way to camp: *You should surely write,* you do not mean *You should write surely,* though it would be nice if the kids' writing showed a little confidence, too.

Placement of adverbs sometimes alters meaning: "I Only Have Eyes for You" (which should read I Have Eyes Only for You, but the song wouldn't have been a hit) is a far semantic cry from Only I Have Eyes for You. You could get lonely from such an abuse of *only.*

Thus, if anybody tells you to avoid preverbs (a neologism for adverbs that come before the verb), hit him with *I always do* or *You never know,* and kayo him by reciting the Gettysburg Address: "The world will little note nor long remember . . ." Sometimes only preverbs will do.

But what of those awful moments when your ear tells you it could go either way? Then follow the fumblerule and stick the adverb at the end; you'll find it works better stylistically. (Which is better than *it stylistically works,* though not so good as a sentence adverb: *Stylistically, it works better.*)

Lean toward using adverbs later; that is all you really need to know. (*Need really?* Nah.)

7

Make an all out effort
to hyphenate
when necessary
but not when
un-necessary.

*I*f you're a male over six feet tall and run a small business, you resent being called a *small businessman* or any other kind of runt. A hyphen can solve the problem: *Small-business man* will work for you. The same solution is available to a slim little woman in a big job who despises sexism in language: She's a *big-business executive,* and if you call her a *big business executive*, you could get slugged with an attaché case.

The hyphen goes all-out to help the writer avoid ambiguity: A *little-known fact* has one meaning; a *little known fact* has two. It directs the reader toward correct pronunciation: Some society editors insist on *rewed* instead of *re-wed,* but that caused one reader to write, "I rewed the day I re-wed him." (That policy will be reformed when sentences are re-formed.) And the hyphen turns two or more words into a unit that becomes a compound adjective: If you like rare meat, a *well-done steak* is not a *steak well done.*

Now we whip around and blaze away at hyphen abuse. Too often, we let the hyphen run a-mok.

Words that end in *ly* are almost always adverbs, and the job of an adverb is to modify an adjective, a verb or another adverb; therefore, a hyphen is not needed to link two modifiers when *ly* is already doing the linking. A nicely handled paragraph is a thing of beauty, and a beautifully unhyphenated combination of adverb and adjective will modify your favorite noun.

A two-word phrase need not be hyphenated

unless you use the phrase as an adjective: "Because the *swing vote* can decide elections, we study *swing-vote* patterns."

When a hyphen is ground down by frequency, let it disappear: Years ago, I took my *girl-friend* to see a show called *The Boy Friend*, but now my old *girlfriend* has found a new *boyfriend*. (Norma Loquendi, what's become of you?)

8

*Don't use Capital letters
without good REASON.*

"*W*hen in the Course of human Events . . ." So begins our declaration of independence, which then goes on to "hold these Truths to be self-evident."

That was the haphazard style of capitalization two centuries ago. No Founding Stylist took Jefferson to task with a brisk "How about we lowercase the *c* in 'Course' and put initial caps on 'human Events,' which seems more important?" Nobody worried about capital letters because not even the new nation had a capital.

Now we do. The trend in capitalizing has been to knock 'em down, at least in the newspaper stylebooks. Plain adjectives and nouns deserve no capital letter, and down comes the *senatorial* privilege, but proper nouns, when referring to a particular place or person, remain standing: the Senate, and Senator Whoosis.

When proper names become parts of general expressions, they get decapitated: Danish, Russian and Turkish become *danish pastry, russian dressing* and *turkish towels*; same when a particular noun becomes general, and *the Constitution* becomes a constitution. (Up in my lead, I tried "declaration of independence," which would be OK for any old declaration of independence, but the specific one in 1776 rates capitals.)

This differentiation can be useful. The Lincoln Memorial is a Washington monument, but the capitalization of the *m* in *Washington Monument* makes it the particular one that looks like a spike. You or I can call ourselves a president and sit in an oval office, but only the President can be found in the Oval Office.

When the decision can go either way—*glass of Burgundy, mother?* or *glass of burgundy, Mother?*—the trick is to make your own decision and stick to it. In this case, I say that *Burgundy* refers to a specific place in which the booze is made, and the *Mother* being addressed is a particular person; to the downsizing stylebookies, I snarl: "Get off my upper case."

9

*It behooves us
to avoid archaisms.*

*W*hen was the last time you felt anything was *incumbent on* you? Did you get up *betimes* this morning, to practice *derring-do?* How long has it been since your arguments were beyond *peradventure* of a doubt?

I delete all e-mail beginning with the word *anent,* because it's a cutesy way of saying *about* (although better than *in reference to*). I am *well-nigh* irritated at folks who can't get the plain *nearly* straight, do not gladly *suffer* fools who use that verb in its original sense of "allow" and never play the game of *perchance.*

These are archaisms, words left over from the Elizabethan era. Fortunately, few of us still use *haply,* meaning "by happenstance, perhaps," because it is so easily confused with *happily.* But some of us do, *withal,* albeit not understandably.

Robert Louis Stevenson, seeking *surcease* from this vocabulary in historical romances, called the practice of exhuming archaisms *tushery.* He was right to deride the pretentious use of dead words: *Parlous,* a dialect corruption of *perilous,* once meant "dangerous" but then became "sneaky" and withered away. Watch out for orators who complain about "these *parlous* times."

When a word dies, pay it a little respect. Don't pick it up. *Behoove* comes from Middle English for "have need of," later gaining a connotation of propriety, and only the C.I.O.'s John L. Lewis, in booming biblical cadence, could get away with "It ill behooves those who have supped at Labor's table . . ."

Stick to *between,* and lay off *betwixt;* you're not *yclept* Beowulf.

Will it bother your prose to lay off archaisms? Not a *whit.*

10

Reserve the apostrophe
for it's proper use
and omit it
when its not needed.

*A*n apostrophe, from the Greek "turning away," is a mark inserted when you turn away from using a letter, as in the typing system of *hunt 'n' peck*.

If I can find the key for the apostrophe on this keyboard, I will illustrate: We use an ' not only when we omit letters in a contraction—*don't come in; we're busy*—but also when we express forms of possession.

Possession is always a problem, even in grammar. If the noun is singular, add an apostrophe and an *s* to form the possessive; if it's plural and ends in *s*, add only the apostrophe. (What'd 'e say?) OK: *Doctor's hours* are for one doctor. *Doctors' hours* are for the bunch of them, with no house calls.

Easy enough—but what do you do about singular words and names ending in *s?* Do you keep up with the *Joneses* or the *Jones'* or the *Jones's?*

Ignore all conflicting advice, of which you can find plenty, and go with me on this: Follow the word ending with *s* with what old rewrite men called *poss ess*. So it's the Court of St. James's, as *The New York Times's* stylebook holds. (When too many sibilant sounds in succession make you sound like a buzz saw, break this rule and write: *Moses' laws, Jesus' steps;* such traditional exceptions are the grammarians' *Achilles' heel.*)

Of course, if the plural does not end in *s*, you don't have to break your head at all; just add the apostrophe and an *s*, as in *women's movement* (never *womens'*).

What about the case of *Its* v. *It's?* Without an

apostrophe, *its* is a possessive pronoun, owning its impenetrability. With the Greek turning-away mark, *it's* is a contraction of *it is* or *it has*.

We only have a certain number of words, and many have to do double duty. It's no use fretting about whose fault it is or who's to blame for its spelling.

11

Write all adverbial forms correct.

*W*hen your fingers are numb with cold, you *feel badly;* when this digital clumsiness causes you to lose the bead-stringing contest, you *feel bad.*

That happy oversimplification leads us into the landscape of flat adverbs, or "fladverbs," mysterious verb modifiers that do not identify themselves with a loud *ly.*

These modifiers are words that sometimes work as adjectives: In *think fast,* the *fast* is an adverb because it modifies a verb, but in the louche lass who used to be the *fast woman, fast* is an adjective modifying the noun *woman.* Same dual use with *hard: hit hard,* adverb, and *hard money,* adjective. Simple? Hardly (adverb, modifying the adjective *simple*).

Let's proceed slowly. Are highway sign painters correct in warning us to *Go Slow?* Are we surely right, or merely colloquial, in saying *You sure fooled me?* Does the moon shine bright on My Old Kentucky Home, or should it shine *brightly?*

You bought this book for answers. Most verbs of sensation and motion take fladverbs: *feel bad, go slow, stop short, taste good* (rather than *taste well,* which is what a wine taster is trained to do). I try to dress spiffily to *look sharp* lest my wife *look sharply* at me.

Other verbs usually take normal adverbs, with the telltale *ly* ending: *sleep soundly, buy cheaply, work quickly,* not to mention *do justly . . . and walk humbly with thy God.*

Look, this sensation-motion directive doesn't cover everything. The sun still idiomatically *shines bright* and adverb freaks are still obliged to *think fast* about *loud/loudly* and *quick/quickly,* but don't feel bad about the occasional ambiguity: If it feels or it moves, drop the *ly* and go for the fladverb. You'll probably be looking sharp and writing correctly.

12

In their writing,
   everyone should make sure
      that their pronouns
   agree with its antecedent.

*E*veryone means "every one" or, put more emphatically, "every single cotton-pickin' *one*."

Although *everyone's* meaning encompasses everybody—six billion people, all the horde of humankind—the indefinite pronoun is construed as singular. Proof: We say, "Everyone is," matching a singular subject with a singular predicate; Norma Loquendi would feel funny saying, "Everyone are."

How can we take a notion of billions and treat it as singular? Easy: it's one collection, one bunch, one crowd.

That's why we match our subject, *everyone*, with its singular pronoun: *his* or *her*, not *their*. If you try to force a singular noun to fit a plural pronoun like *their* or *our*, you may get some support from long-dead authors like Henry Fielding, but present-day users of the language will wince. Stick to the correct "Everyone does *his* thing."

Hold on—isn't that sexist? Why *his* and not *her?*

OK, then use *her* instead of *his* every other time, as some Supreme Court justices do. Or play it safe with fairness and feminism by matching *everyone* (or *anyone* or *everybody* or *either the one or the other*) with *his or her.*

But, you say, that's awkward—too obviously straining not to offend. One way out is to emulate hotshot Broadway producers who find themselves in awkward positions with their stars: Recast.

Instead of freezing on starting with *Everybody,* start your sentence with *People* or *All whatsits.* Thus, you avoid the mistaken "Everybody pick up their keys at the desk" by saying, "All tenants pick up their keys at the desk" or—if you wish to avoid both sexism and solecism while stressing the imperative mood—"Pick up your damn keys by noon or you'll be locked out forever."

You own the sentence; the sentence doesn't own you. To wriggle out of awkward concessions to sexism or anti-sexism, rewrite the fumblerule to: "All of us, in our writing, should make our pronouns agree with their antecedents." But then it wouldn't be a fumblerule, and you'd forget.

13

Use the semicolon properly,
use it between complete
but related thoughts;
and not between an
independent clause and
a mere phrase.

*I*n the 70s, the dash was hot—it expressed the herky-jerkiness of the age of insertion and after-thought. In the 80s and 90s, the ellipsis became the rage, because its three dots in mid-sentence (or four dots at the end) showed the spoken word dominating the written word . . . dribbling off dreamily. . . .

In the nameless first decade of the third millennium, we're moving toward connectedness; buy semicolon stock. Unlike the period, which decisively separates complete thoughts, or the comma, which gently separates phrases, the semicolon is the Cleopatra of punctuation marks; she separates and connects at the same time, making hungry where most she satisfies.

Granted, this tease of a mark has her mundane uses. She provides separation, and averts confusion, in a list of phrases that contain commas within the phrases. "Here come our adversary, the dictatorial leader; our champion, the American President; and a horde of aides drawn up in vast, cumbrous array." Without those semicolons, that stately parade of phrases becomes a mob of words.

But what gives this baby sex appeal is the way she pushes clauses apart while holding them together. That makes her the handmaiden of the slanting linkers; when *nevertheless, furthermore, besides, however* and such conjunctive adverbs demand entry into a sentence, they need a half-stopper in front of them to ensure their independence.

Never waste a semicolon's talents on mere coordinating conjunctions, such as *and, but, or.* Instead, make a choice: Write "I'm right and you're wrong" or "I'm right; you're wrong." Either is right, but "I'm right; and you're wrong" is wrong.

We've all been taught that a semicolon is less of a pause than a period and more than a comma, but that misses the subtlety of its use.

In some cases, you will want a burst of short sentences to make your declaration punchy; at other times, you will use a string of commas, rhythmically, repetitiously, to make your point; though, when the moment comes, to link ideas without fully merging them, to engage in the trial marriage of thoughts— make a dash for the semicolon.

14

Don't use no double negatives.

"*I* . . . ain't got no bah-dee . . . ," goes the lyric, in an intentional double negative. To be correct, it would go, "I ain't got any bah-dee" or, to the applause of grammatical stiffs, "I have no bah-dee."

A double negative is described by some, with a discreet cough, as "nonstandard." In truth, it is a mistake. Error. Solecism. Don't never do it nohow, unless you're spoofin'.

But what of the *not un-* construction, often accompanied by a lifted pinkie and a world-weary sigh? "I am *not unmindful* of the double negatives used by our more unfortunate brethren . . ." Is that a double negative?

It is not only that, but an affectation to boot. Although *not un-* is not incorrect (OK, it's correct, because the two negatives reinforce each other to make a weak positive), the la-di-da construction is arch, weak and fuzzy.

Sometimes *not un-* cannot be avoided: If somebody asks if you're happy and you're not, but you don't want to be a drag, then it is accurate enough to lie about your mood as *not unhappy.* Better form, to avoid being the skunk at the garden party, would be to pretend you're *moderately happy,* or more subtly, *happy enough.*

This is what the Greeks called *litotes,* pronounced LIGHT-oh-tease, which has come to mean "understatement for effect." When I offend traditionalists by accepting the word *hopefully,* I expect to get not a few irate e-mails; in this sentence, *not a few* really means "a whole bundle," and I am employing litotes, and being cute.

As you can see, the high-class double negative is as bad, in my book, as the low-class double negative, but in both cases—as in "I ain't got no bah-dee"— occasional use for specific effect is not unreasonable.

15

Also, avoid all awkward or
affected alliteration.

*H*ow can I, the ghostly author of "nattering nabobs of negativism," knock the device of alliteration? Here's how: Ostracize overboard orators.

Repeating the same first sound, consonant or vowel, is a trick to make a phrase memorable. It worked for orators long before what Charles Churchill called "apt alliteration's artful aid." (That, by the way, is an example of mere visual alliteration—the alliterative trick is primarily one of sound, not sight, and at least three of those *a*'s are pronounced differently.)

The rhetorical device is undeniably powerful. Chaucer first used the simile "brown as a berry," a phrase that owes its survival through six centuries to alliteration only, despite the plain fact that berries are more often red or blue than brown. Same mystery with "dead as a doornail," which has long driven etymologists up the wall, causing lexicographers to grumble, "Origin obscure." Israelis who did not like the connotation of Jerusalem's "Wailing Wall" changed it to "Western Wall," fixing the image without touching the alliteration.

Trouble comes when you take it too far. President Harding's "not nostrums but normalcy" was fine, especially considering his use of a nice variant of *normality,* but consider the rest of that passage: "not revolution but restoration, not agitation but adjustment, not surgery but serenity, not the dramatic but the dispassionate, not experiment but equipoise . . ."

Come on, now; that was accurately described as "bloviation" (an Americanism combining "blow-hard" with "deviation"), and serves as a warning to aspiring alliterators: Lay off too much of a good thing.

Straining for effect produces the effect of affectation. Only if speakers use alliteration like salt, sprinkling it sparingly, will we wary writers witness the rightful return of ringing rhetoric.

16

When a dependent clause
precedes an independent
clause put a comma after
the dependent clause.

*S*ay what you like about the Founding Fathers—they knew what to do after dependent clauses.

"When, in the Course of human events, it becomes necessary for one people to dissolve the political bands which have connected them with another"—we're still in that first dependent clause—"and to assume among the Powers of the earth the separate and equal station to which the Laws of Nature and of nature's God entitle them," (whew! the comma after *them* marks the end of the dependent clause; now here comes the independent clause of the Declaration of Independence) "a decent respect to the opinions of mankind requires that they should declare the causes which impel them to the separation."

Time tends to erode great principles. Young patriots today think nothing of saying, "When I go you go"—leaving out the comma after the first *go*—or "If you can't pick it up paint it." This refusal to pause after a dependent clause or even to signify a vestigial interest in a pause by sticking in a comma lets down the side.

When dealing with a thought that precedes your big thought (as I do here, comma) set it off with a little pause represented by the comma. The thought in your independent, or main, clause will then hit all the harder.

Give your main clause a little space. Prose is not like boxing; the skilled writer deliberately telegraphs his punch, knowing that the reader wants to take the message directly on the chin.

Dependent clauses begin with subordinators like *after, unless, because, provided;* yes, like any introductory words (like *yes, like*), these clauses set up the payoff; without the comma, the clauses run together and you miss the point.

To come to that point, remember this: If it moves, salute it.

17

If I've told you once,
I've told you
a thousand times:
Resist hyperbole.

"*I* could eat a horse, couldn't you?"

"No, but I'd kill for a cup of coffee."

Hyperbole began when a little kid in ancient Greece wound up and heaved a ball farther than anybody thought he could. That was *hyperballein,* from *hyper,* "over" or "beyond," and *ballein,* meaning "throw," as in tossing a ball.

The kid must have had some arm. (I'd give my right arm for an arm like that.) The word *hyperbole* came to mean "intended excess," exaggeration designed to emphasize so wildly as not to mislead. The poet William Blake, who held infinity in the palm of his hand, was using the same device; so is the unctuous waiter who offers "a thousand pardons" when you tell him, "We've been waiting forever."

The trick to effective hyperbole is to give an original twist to obviously fanciful overstatement. "I'd walk a million miles for one of your smiles" would no longer impress Mammy, but Raymond Chandler's "She was blonde enough to make a bishop kick a hole through a stained-glass window" still has that crisp crunch of freshness.

How about *hype,* as in the sort of *media hype* that turns a minor irritation into a national firestorm overnight—is that a shortening of *hyperbole?*

No, that's folk etymology, and the folk are always wrong. That *hype* comes from "hypodermic needle," the shortening of which was lifted out of narcotics lingo by the showman Billy Rose in 1950 when he wrote of "no fake suspense, no hyped-up glamour." The compound adjective *hyped-up* eventually became the noun *hype*.

Although both *hype* and *hyperbole* mean "exaggeration," the first means "sensationalism with intent to bamboozle, or at least to shock or impress," while the old Greek word still is free of any connotation of phoniness. Classy writers will not indulge in *hype* for all the tea in China.

18

*If any word is improper
at the end of a sentence,
a linking verb is.*

*H*ere's the secret to sentences: Don't start them fuzzily, and don't dribble off at the end. To be specific, avoid boring beginnings like *It is* or *There are* and eschew wimpish conclusions such as linking verbs, and like that. (*And like that* is a classic dribble-off.)

What's a linking verb, and why should you have to know about it? A linking verb (as in *to be, to seem* and the sense verbs *to feel, to smell,* etc.) holds together, or links, the subject to the zingy part of your sentence— the noun that explains or the adjective that describes the subject and gives the sentence a purpose.

In the sentence *I am a language maven,* I is the subject, *am* is the linking verb and *maven* is the noun that explains what *I* is (which grammarians call the predicate nominative and etymologists call a Yiddishism).

In the sentence *I feel sick when you start with that "predicate nominative" stuff,* the subject is *I* and the zingy bit is *sick,* which describes the green look of the subject; the linking verb is *feel.*

Why does any sensible person have a need to know this? The reason this information is useful is that we have now demonstrated such words as *is* and *becomes* to be a fulcrum. To the playground: When the fulcrum is in the middle, you get motion at both ends of the seesaw; in the same way, when the linking verb is where it belongs, you get a bright opener and a strong conclusion.

Go try to operate a seesaw with the fulcrum on

either end—only that end moves, and you could get a hernia. Same thing when your linking verb is at the end; you've contracted terminal dribble-off. Depressed is how you feel. (With the linking verb where it belongs, *You feel depressed* is what that becomes. Now recast the preceding sentence and put *becomes* where it belongs.)

None of this applies to questions. *It's 10 P.M.—do you know where your predicate nominative is?* If you do, tell it that *Home is where the heart is.*

19

Avoid commas,
  that are not necessary.

*C*ommas can change meanings. A Texas legislator addressed a youthful audience and sought to ingratiate himself with "We are of like minds," and some students understood him to say, "We are of, like, minds."

Place your pauses with care. Richard Nixon once set off a furor about politicizing the Supreme Court by introducing "that great Republican Chief Justice, Earl Warren." A more careful placement of the pause would have changed the word being modified from the name of the job to the name of the man, as in "that great Republican, Chief Justice Earl Warren."

A comma signals a pause, which in turn signifies a separation. The sentence you just read needed the pause after *pause,* because a non-defining clause was being introduced, and those clauses that do not define words in the main body of the sentence need all the set-off support they can get.

Defining clauses, on the other hand, need no comma crutches: The previous paragraph could have begun, "A comma signals a pause that signifies a separation," which would have saved a comma and some ink, but I inserted that , *which in turn* to put a little space between the signal and the signification.

Remember Dracula: When you see a *which,* hold a mirror up to drive it back by making the mark of the comma.

Don't use commas to splice thoughts that can stand by themselves; use semicolons instead, like this. Don't use a comma when *and* is doing the linking of short clauses: *Do me a favor and drop dead* is stronger when comma-free.

Do use commas for *this, that, and the other thing,* being sure to put a comma before the final *and* in series when there is danger of confusion in fusing the last two items.

Every comma requires a pause, but not every pause requires a comma. You are permitted some wiggle room in this comma business. Let the reader decide now and then; you're the writer, not the director.

20

*Verbs has to agree
with their subjects.*

*E*verybody and his brother knows that a singular subject ("Everybody") takes a singular verb ("knows"). But how about compound subjects such as "Everybody and his brother"?

I just painted myself into an inescapable corner, because I used an idiom that intentionally kicks proper grammar in the head. Try again: Compound subjects tied together by *and* are plural and take plural verbs: "My brother and I know everything."

However, compound subjects joined by *or* take the number of the subject nearest the verb: "All my correspondents or I am right," but "I or all my correspondents are right." If you can't be near the subject you love, agree with the subject you're near.

McCall's magazine had an ad campaign with pictures of such exciting women as Tina Turner and Carly Simon captioned "One of the drab homebodies who reads *McCall's*." When grammarians groaned, the editor put the decision to me: Was *one of the drab homebodies* to be construed as singular, with the central meaning *one* (calling for *who reads*) or construed as plural, with the central meaning *the drab homebodies* (calling for *who read*)?

I lingered over those pictures. The essence of the subject was the *bodies*, not the *one*, and proximity to the verb also lent its weight. I ruled the subject to be plural; it followed that the verb also had to be plural:

who read. The magazine had to tear down a great many posters, but decisions can be Draconian in the language dodge.

21

*Avoid trendy locutions
that sound flaky.*

*I*f you try a little too hard to be with it, you're out of it.

The *glitterati* was a good play on "glittering literati" when it was first used in the late 30s, but it's a stale word today; same with *biggie,* as in *media biggie,* who gets *megabucks* for writing *page-turners* or *books with legs* that presumably walk off shelves but are not really *good reads.*

In the sixties, academics made *viable* their own, and politicians made *option* their only choice, until somebody wrote that "suicide is a viable option," and that put the kibosh on both of them. (*Kibosh,* from the Irish for "cap of death," is so formerly trendy that it qualifies as informal usage.)

In the 70s, professional football contributed the verb *blindside* and the nouns *cheap shot* and *judgment call,* while Carterites talked *flat-out* of *zero error* and *power curve* until Mr. Reagan *did a number on* Mr. Carter.

In the 80s, the *L-word* (for *liberal*) was chosen to be overdone, with its derivative *A-question* about adultery too liberally asked. Teens clipped *disrespect* to *dis* and made it a verb, while the first President George Bush introduced baby talk to the political vocabulary with *deep doo-doo.*

Review the above and ask yourself: Would you use any of those locutions today without being conscious of being *so* twentieth century? In formal writing, all such jargon or slang must be squeezed for freshness before using.

In casual speech, a word like *flaky*—from baseball slang, for an off-the-wall character—can nicely spice the lingo, but never force it. You can wrinkle your nose and say, *"Gross!"*, expecting some kid to take you for a Valley Girl, when that word has been long replaced by the negative *gnarly, ill* or even *from hell*.

Language mavens are allowed to use words like *maven* in formal writing because that's our *shtick*.

22

"The male pronoun
embraces the female"
is a nonsexist standard
that should be
followed by all
humankind.

*D*artmouth College, after fourteen years of coeducation, changed the name of the song "Men of Dartmouth" to something thought to be less sexist. The choice: "Alma Mater," which has syllables that fit the notes but is Latin for "Fostering Mother"; male freshpersons were appalled.

The too-determined use of *person* to replace *man,* as in *chairperson* for the old *chairman,* rightly drew ridicule: Was the *mailman* to be called the *personperson?* Proponents of nonsexist usage drew back a bit: For a time the person who chaired a meeting was called the Chair, a stretch of the ancient metaphor "to take the Chair."

When a noun blatantly discriminates against women, change the word to avoid offense. One day many women will bear as well as wear hose; therefore, *fireman* is becoming *firefighter,* just as *policeman* and *lawman* have become *police officer.*

Heaven no longer protects the woiking goil; change *workingman* to *worker* (not the bloodless *personnel*). The same concern for a sense of equality and fairness is why *congressman* is on the way out; newspapers have come to title the members of that house *representatives.*

Now we come to the controversy: what about the pronoun? For centuries, it has been *he,* when *he or she* was meant; must we now, in the name of fairness, ostentatiously alternate the usage or use both and thereby give brevity a shot in the teeth? Must "everybody should watch his language" now become "everybody should watch *his or her* language," or worse, "*their* language"?

Etymologists know that the word *man,* going back to the Sanskrit *manus,* means "human being" and is sexless. Although *man* and *woman* are differentiated in English, the universal meaning of *man* to encompass both sexes remains. Why accept a fiat from anti-sexism headquarters to change it now?

Cool it, humankind; let the language change in its own time, not to fit the schedule of any -ism. Resist the linguistic importunings of those who say, "Get with it, man."

23

*And don't start a sentence
with a conjunction.*

"*A*nd the earth was without form, and void." That's from the second verse of Genesis, in the translation into English by some of King James's heavy hitters.

"And the war came." That is the saddest short sentence Abraham Lincoln ever wrote, resonant with resignation.

And that's not all, as the pitchmen say. (Out-of-date pitchmen, that is; those on the cusp prefer *plus*.) The usagist Fowler found no error in beginning a sentence with *and*. He derided any objection to the practice as "a faintly lingering superstition."

Why, then, do we feel that frisson of guilt when we start a sentence with *and, but* or *because?*

Because God, not long after letting there be light, put conjunctions in the world for the purpose of conjoining—to connect, couple and link—and not primarily to introduce. Just as nouns name, adjectives describe and verbs act, conjunctions (and prepositions) connect or subordinate; that's their essence. This paragraph begins with a sentence fragment, not a stylish complete sentence, a trap we often fall into when starting with *because*.

So it's incorrect to start a sentence with a conjunction? No; it's OK. (What is incorrect is to use *so* as a conjunction in formal speech.) But when you do, you often seem to be using a half-sentence. And when you follow it with another half-sentence, you get this sort of choppy effect. When you want a cup of coffee, it's silly to order two demitasses.

When is a good time to start with *and*? Suppose you want to give the impression of not beginning at the beginning. Shirley Jackson began a great short story with "And the first thing they did was segregate me." Because it has a dramatic effect, it works, as *because* does in this sentence; the opening conjunctions can deliver starkness.

And yes, I confess to using them myself, when I want to suggest a seeming afterthought, or to pose as if dragging an admission out of myself that I had not planned to set forth at the start.

But don't do it too often. Because it hits hard. And prose can get punch-drunk.

24

The passive voice
should never be used.

"*I* was the recipient of a million dollars. My wife was awarded the Nobel prize. My children were educated in the school of hard knocks."

All these are passive constructions, so called because the subject of each sentence is lying there, lollygagging flat on his back, receiving the action passively. My purpose is to focus on the recipients, leading each sentence with them, which is why I use the passive voice. In effect, I made the objects the subjects.

If I wanted to focus on the real subjects and transmit the action directly to the object, I would use the active voice: "A million dollars landed on my neck, the Nobel prize pleased hell out of my wife and the school of hard knocks educated my kids."

Writers write books; that's active, with my subject (writers) transmitting action (writing) to the object (books, or in some cases software). *Books are written by writers* is passive, emphasizing my old object (books) by turning it into the subject, and slightly derogating writers by making each of them an object, as so often happens in real life.

I say that those are good uses of passivity. However, the bad use of the passive voice is in obfuscation. Abraham Lincoln, to escape personal responsibility in a message to Congress, changed all the active voices to passive, and bureaucrats have been following that example ever since.

Permission was refused is the classic trick in passive construction; it avoids the need for a perpetrator of the turn-down. In the active voice, the writer would have to say, *Joe Blow refused permission*—but Mr. Blow may not want the responsibility. That's why this device is favored in diplomatic documents.

Be forceful; use the active voice. Now and then, however, it is considered advisable to use the passive when the need presents itself to crawl under the desk. That's when the forthright "I made a mistake" is fuzzed up to "Mistakes were made."

25

Writing carefully, dangling participles should be avoided.

"*S*peaking as an old friend," began Richard Nixon, "there has been a disturbing tendency in statements from Beijing . . ."

I winced; my old boss was dangling a participial phrase. To some, dangling a participial is as bad as mangling a marsupial (as in smacking a wombat); to others, this abuse of a modifier is tolerated as one of the oldest and most frequent mistakes in the language. To me, allowing a phrase to float without visible means of support is annoying because it's confusing.

Back to basics: A participle is a swinging verb form that can do almost anything in grammar. In its present tense alone, with the familiar *ing* ending, it can carry action like a verb (*let's go swinging*). It can also take a noun's shape and call itself a gerund (*swinging can get you in trouble, buddy*), and it can modify like an adjective or adverb (*a swinging party can make a landlord raving mad*).

That last trick of the participle, acting as a modifier, is what troubles some writers. They leave it hanging out there without making it modify a subject.

"Speaking candidly," Mr. Nixon went on, "I believe some of our Chinese friends have misunderstood . . ." Now, that was correct: The participial phrase *Speaking candidly* is attached to the subject, *I*; earlier, when he was using *Speaking as an old friend,* he forgot the subject and launched into *there has been a disturbing tendency.*

Whenever a participial phrase is followed by *it* or *there,* watch out. Never forget the subject; not only would it be wrong, but it also might mislead the reader.

Jacques Barzun, the great grammarian, produced the classic example of the dangle with the funny angle: "Quickly summoning an ambulance, the corpse was carried to the mortuary." Always ask: Who did the action? Put another way, where's the subject?

After setting forth this indisputable rule, it should be clear . . . (No. Try again.) Having made this point, the reader will never again make the mistake of . . . (No. If *the reader* is to be the subject, the preceding phrase, referring to the writer, is kicking its feet in midair.) Knowing the danger of dangling, the astute writer will . . .

Now we've got it.

26

Unless you are quoting other people's exclamations, kill all exclamation points!!!

*T*he exclamation mark is in disrepute. Ever since F. Scott Fitzgerald advised, "Cut out all those exclamation points. An exclamation point is like laughing at your own joke," writers have accepted the notion that the punchy little mark is un-cool.

Wait! Don't kill that useful little stage direction. Some readers need all the help they can get from the author, and the EP can reflect the emphasis intended by an interjection.

We must listen soberly to all the warnings against excessive exclaiming. Never use a punctuation mark to prop up a weak exclamation ("Gee!" he ejaculated) or to hype a mild emotion (He was real cute!). Never, never, never use exclamation points in series—!!!—which gets a triple-X rating in the punctilio of punctuation. Never use the EP at the end of a long sentence.

But consider prose without the EP: Whew, that's a relief. White whale off the starboard bow. Stop, thief. Help, I'm drowning. Hold that line. Storm the Bastille. OK, language pundit—gotcha. Don't these sentences, denuded of their EP, seem flat, listless and missing something?

You bet! (No. That's an example of abusing the EP to add unwarranted enthusiasm.)

When you are interjecting a word or phrase to express horror *(aargh!)*, disgust *(yecch!)*, fear *(gulp!)* or triumph *(ah-hah!)*, the absence of an exclamation mark will be remarked.

Another use of the point is in lieu of "just listen to this," or "look who's talking," interpolated parenthetically, as in "My five-year-old announced she wanted a milk bath (!)." In this use, the EP is as short an editorial comment as you can find.

Do you want your interjection to explode? If your answer is "Hell, no!", then—heavens to Betsy—don't use the exclamation point.

27

*Never use a long word
when a diminutive one
will do.*

A senator groping for a more elegant word than *wording* rose to say, "The *verbiage* can be argued, but . . ."

That's one danger in choosing an unfamiliar word: The offbeat can be off-base. *Verbiage* once meant "a style of diction" but, influenced by *foliage,* it has leafed out to mean "the product of bloviation and logorrhea."

Holdit. *Verbiage* has come to mean "wordiness," which is truer and more widely understandable than the other forty-dollar specials used in the preceding definition.

Many of us like to stretch the minds of our readers, introducing them to the big menu behind the list of daily word specials, but all too often we practice polysyllabicism because we want to show off. Lookame, I got this prodigious vocabulary.

Why did I choose *prodigious* just now? Why not the first word that came to mind: *big?* Because it wasn't big enough. Then why not *immense, mammoth, colossal?* Too common, and shrunken in meaning by olive packagers.

The only others I could think of were *gargantuan,* which has a large-animal connotation and is unsuitable for intellectual boasting; *humongous* (a recent amalgam of *huge* and *enormous* used mainly by kids); and *prodigious,* which combines size with amazement.

The best choice would have been *huge.* Little word, slam-bang impact. Would have had a nice ironic twist, modifying *vocabulary* with a short word that consciously avoids the arcane. Sorry, it didn't come to me.

What came to me is what could come to you: a thesaurus on a word processor. Just put the cursor on a word, hit a pair of buttons and survey the feast of synonyms.

The danger is that you will show off by picking the big ones: *asseverate* for *assert*.

Resist. In this brave computer world, choose the word that says precisely what you mean. In that way, you will avoid the animadversions of your friends.

28

The rigid rule of
   "i before e except after c"
      raises spelling
   to a sceince.

*P*retend you see a mouse, jump on a chair and yell, "Eek!" Observe the spelling of that piercing sound of *ee;* that's the simple way, with a double *e,* as in *seek a peek.* The other, more complicated and unfortunately necessary way is with an *ie,* as in *piercing.*

When you are called upon to use that complicated way, signify that squealing sound in writing by putting *i* in front of *e*—which will yield relief rather than grief from your chief niece in the field.

Except, of course, when the *ee* sound comes after a *c:* then it will be your conceit to perceive a deceiving ceiling. The exception to this exception is *science,* and at this point most people conclude that spelling rules don't help much.

They do help some. With your brain stuffed with the above—*i* before *e* except after *c,* when you're shrieking at the mouse—consider the other side of that coin. How do you handle the *i* and the *e* when the mouse is gone and the sound is different from the *ee* in *eeking?*

Easy; spell it the other way around, with the *i* after the *e.* That goes for the "eye" sound, as in the beer-drinker's command, "Heighten that stein." Also for the "ih" sound, as in the protectionist derogation: "Foreign heifers are counterfeit." And the *e* also comes before the *i* for the long "a" sound, as in the cheerful winter-time order: "Weigh my sleigh, neighbor."

That will help you, as it does me, most of the

time. Not all the time. Only the other day I had occasion to shout, "Seize the sheik, friend, before he does further mischief!" That's one way to keep track of the damned exceptions.

As Karl Marx never wrote: "Spellers of the world, untie!"

29

Proofread carefully
to see if you
any words out.

*T*he all-too-honest-typographer's laurel wreath was given to the Montvale, New Jersey, homeowner who advertised a "Specious Ranch on One Acre"; runner-up was the Chinese restaurant in Rockville, Maryland, for the shuddering impact of its "Authentic Human Cuisine."

Intending to use *powderpuff* as a sneering attributive noun, I wrote it *powerpuff;* readers immediately accused me of a linguistic powderplay. The truth is I left out a letter. (The greater truth is *that* I just left out a word.)

The Treasury Department sent out a mailing beginning, "Official Bussiness." Six million copies went out before some nitpicker's complaint got through.

Here's the best way to proofread copy: Get somebody else to do it. If necessary, do it with them, reading aloud to each other, pronouncing *the* as "thee" and not "thuh," pronouncing the pronunciation marks (open parenthesis, even though it slows you down, close parenthesis).

Adopt a posture of humility before all written copy: You may think your eyes are sharp, but nothing beats a different pair of eyes. If you write a mistake, or commit a misspelling or leave out a word, that mistake is lurking inside your head, and you are the last person to find it on the paper.

If you are a hermit, do not proofread immediately after writing. Let the mistake slip out of your brain overnight. Fresh eyes will help, even when they are your own.

Be sure to see your stuff in print; somehow, it looks different from type, or the gleaming words on a computer screen. In print, you can spot how your intended *recused* has become *rescued,* and you still have time to save the day.

Above all, check for *not's.* Whenever you see *now,* ask yourself: Should this be a *not?* When your meaning is negative, ask: Where's my *not?* Some words left out will merely cause embarrassment; others will clap you in the for perjury.

30

Use parallel structure
when you write
and in speaking.

"*W*atch what we do, not what we say." That beautiful balance of clauses by an old politician deserves our salute, his subsequent incarceration notwithstanding. The same thought, expressed with nouns in balance, goes, "Deeds, not words."

We could say, "Watch what we do, not words," but it would be wrong. So would "Deeds, not what we say." The phrases offend the ear and confuse the mind because they knock the balance skewhiffy.

Consider the previous sentence, quivering in perfect symmetry at the end of the last paragraph. *Offend the ear* is parallel to *confuse the mind,* and both run along the same verb-article-noun track as *knock the balance.*

Now kick that sentence's structure around: "The phrases *offend the ear* and are *confusing to the mind* because the *balance was knocked* skewhiffy." To derogate that messed-up sentence in perfect parallel: It is a hodgepodge of tenses, a farrago of endings, a muddle of phrases.

When a writer uses parallel structure, he helps the reader sort out the meaning of a complex idea. He tells his word troops to march in step because the crisp discipline contributes to clarity.

The trick is to repeat an introductory word before each phrase or verb or noun in parallel: I love *to* woo, *to* wed, *to* wander, *to* pay alimony. No word breaks ranks. I am *in* love, *in* wedded bliss, *in* trouble, *in* hock.

See how this device can be used in phrasemaking. Speaker Sam Rayburn said of President Harry Truman: "Right on all the big things, wrong on most of the little ones." The *right* and the *big* match the *wrong* and the *little;* it would be rhetorically silly to say, "Right on all the big things, angry at all the journalists."

Come, see, conquer; parallelism is easy to write, is simple to understand, and you sometimes can break the rhythm for effect.

31

Boycott eponyms.

*D*r. Thomas Bowdler, eager to make Shakespeare "fit for the perusal of our virtuous females," cut out what he considered the naughty and profane words. In his sanitized version, Lady Macbeth's "Out, damn'd spot!" was changed to "Out, crimson spot!", which earned the censor a place in the dictionaries in the verb *to bowdlerize.*

We use two types of eponyms: overt and covert. (*Covert*'s first syllable, once pronounced "kuh," is now "koh"—to match the "oh" in *overt.*)

Overt eponyms are names that many of us know have been turned into words. The Earl of Cardigan and the Earl of Sandwich could have had a cozy lunch. Samuel Maverick and his contemporary, James Bowie, are widely known as the sources of the rambunctious cattle and the curved knife. Louis Braille invented his writing system and Richard Bright identified his kidney disease. (Groucho Marx once said, "I've got Bright's Disease, but not to worry—he's got mine.")

The Reverend William Spooner gave his name to the switching of letters, as in *tons of soil* for *sons of toil,* or the inversion of words, as in a recent president's observation of his intent "to look back and sit at the world." And who can forget the hated landlord's agent, Captain Charles Boycott, and the beloved feminist Amelia Bloomer?

Those are all fairly well-known eponyms (Greek for "upon a name"). Less remarked are the place names whose original identities have faded, as did Lord Baltimore's city in Queen Mary's land. Even murkier are people almost forgotten: Derrick was a seventeenth-century English hangman and William Lynch an eighteenth-century American vigilante.

From the fright of nymphs at the sudden appearance of the god Pan comes *panic,* according to one version of the etymology; from the name of the Titan whose picture supporting the world was placed on the title page of Mercator's first book of maps comes *atlas;* from Augustus Caesar, who liked the way his great-uncle Julius named the month of *July* after himself, comes *August;* from the muttonchop whiskers of an unsuccessful Union general named Burnside, *sideburns.*

Try not to load up a sentence with overt eponymous words; that's like delivering a draconian decision in a stentorian voice.

32

Ixnay on colloquial stuff.

*I*f you are with a bunch of stiffs and feel the need to describe your physical state, you should express yourself with the Standard English *I'm tired* rather than the colloquial *I'm beat* or the slang *I'm really dragging my ass.*

The latter two locutions are neither profane nor obscene; they are surely more forceful and heartfelt, but they are out of place. That's the question about colloquialisms: not "Is this correct?" but "Is it correct here and now, in front of these people?"

Time was, *colloquial* was thought of as "low-class." A colloquy is a conversation, and the spoken word has lower standards than the written word; to get away from the pejorative connotation, lexicographers took to using *informal* to describe such colloquialisms as *get it* for *understand.*

The language reflects the culture, which is changing; informality is in. (*In,* a colloquialism, is in; *into,* as in "He's into porn," is still slang and may never get in.) Words like *informal, relaxed, casual, breezy, easygoing* have it all over (or easily dominate) words like *standard, formal, conventional, stately.*

That gives *colloquial* a new connotation and colloquial language a wider acceptance. You are not a relativist wimp if you go with this flow; context has always affected meaning, and the ready acceptance of *wimp* (from *whimper*) and *go with the flow* (from surfers' lingo) requires a new look at the meaning of "standard."

The center of vocabulary gravity has shifted. Slang—deliberately ephemeral cant, colorful vulgarity, argot designed to shock or to limit understanding to those who know the code—is still clearly nonstandard, but the line between *colloquial* and *standard* is disappearing.

"Enjoy," says the waitress, in an unconscious use of a Yiddishism. A decade ago, that was colloquial; now you hear it from the most elegant captain at New York's Four Seasons.

Same with the language; enjoy.

33

*Of all the rules about
indefinite pronouns,
none is useful.*

*W*hat does the indefinite pronoun *none* mean to you?

When it means "not one," you'll write *none is;* when it means "not any," you'll write *none are.*

That's heresy to the hidebound. They like the old rule that held, *"None* is construed as singular."

That was the way it used to be (and try not to end a sentence with a linking verb). When John Dryden wrote, "None but the brave deserves the fair," his *deserves* shows he thought of *none* as "not one."

But Dryden is dead, and none of his buddies are alive. If today we treat *none* as plural, none dare call it treason.

Today *none* is most often used to mean "not any" or, generally, "not ones." Therefore, none of us are wrong to construe *none* as plural, and to say *none have, none go, none waltz.*

Wait a second; *None waltz* sounds funny. Isn't that phrase's sense really "Nobody waltzes anymore"? Shouldn't it then be the singular *None waltzes?*

Look: If you mean *nobody, not one person, not a single individual*—if you have the singular clearly in your mind—then use *nobody* or *not one.* Save *none* for when you are thinking negatively of several ("not any of them") or of a non-quantity ("none of it").

Don't get hung up on collectives. *A few of us* is a collective phrase, and such a bunch is technically singular, but it is absurd to think of "a few" as one. It's never *a few of us was;* it's always "a few of us were."

Here's how to remember how to treat the indefinite pronoun: Get definite in your own mind about the number. If one, then *Nobody is perfect.* If a few, or an all-encompassing multitude, then *None of us are perfect.*

34

Zap onomatopoeia.

*A*strophysicists have a *big bang* theory to explain the origin of the universe. Linguists have a *bow-wow* theory to explain the origin of language, holding that speech originated in man's imitation of the grunts and growls of animals.

Bang and *bow-wow*—along with such razzmatazz words as *buzz, bash, bop, sizzle* and *crash*—are examples of *onomatopoeia,* a lilting word formed from the Greek *onoma,* "name," and *poios,* "making."

From the tintinnabulary *ring-a-ling* to the more recent *ding-a-ling,* words coined from the sounds of what they describe enliven and enrich the language.

Reduplicators love it: *Teeny-weeny* is the squeaky sound of something small, *mumbo-jumbo* an incomprehensible murmur. *Hee-haw* and *seesaw* evoke the ass and the bouncing posterior; *flip-flop* was originally the sound of a flounder on the deck, and is now the sound of a political reassessment; and *zigzag* is a visual onomatopoeia, imitating the movement of the *z's.*

Should we resist? When our children point a finger at us and say lovingly, "Zap, you're dead!", should we treat *zap* as a nonce term or include it in our dictionaries as new Standard English?

Include it (but don't include it *in*). *Zap* was first used in the late 1920s by Philip Francis Nowlan, the creator of the comic-strip character Buck Rogers, to describe the sound made by his paralysis gun.

Since then, this onomatopoeic specimen has

come to mean, first, "to kill with a burst of gunfire or electric current," then more happily "to avoid or delete television commercials with a remote-control erasure," one of life's more rewarding pleasures. *Zap,* the verb, has filled society's need of a jocular term for "to destroy, annihilate, pulverize."

Here goes: *Zap!,* you're standard.

35

*Resist new verb forms
that have snuck
    into the language.*

"*L*ast time up at bat," said the sportscaster, "he flew out."

Wrong. This is an example of incorrect correction, just as *spit 'n' image* is miscorrected to *spitting image* by wrongheaded pedants.

When a baseball batter hits a fly ball that is caught, the past tense of his action is *flied out.* Only if he then dropped his bat, flapped his arms and soared out of the stadium could he be hoo-hahed as one who *flew out.*

We have gotten tensed up about verb forms for good reason: Some past tenses have been twisted out of shape. I *get* abuse; I *got* tough; as a result, I *have gotten* too much mail. The trouble is, the past participle of *get* is either *got* or *gotten,* which is confusing. Don't swim with the descriptivists; strike a blow for clarity by saying *gotten* after *have.*

You say you've swum with those roundheels of language before? Good for you—the past participle of *swim* is *swum,* and *have swum* is well above water, but remember the past tense is *swam.* ("You swam the moat?")

Snuck is dialect, a century-old Southernism. The proper past tense of *sneak* is *sneaked,* but the analogy of *strike/struck, sink/sank/sunk, stink/stank/stunk, shrink/ shrank/shrunk* and *swim/swam/swum* is strong: We all have an urge to use a *u* in the furthest past tense.

I say stick with *sneaked* in formal settings—"Yer

Honor, the poipetrator sneaked past all of us"—but go with *snuck* when you want to be loose and colorful: "This recession snuck up on us."

The past tense of *sneak* may someday clash with the past tense of the newer verb *to snack,* but that's for our kids to worry about.

36

*Better to walk through
the valley of the shadow
of death than to string
prepositional phrases.*

*W*ith regard to prepositional phrases, good writers strike out *with regard to, with reference to, on account of, by means of, as regards* and *with the exception of.*

These are boilerplate phrases, guaranteed MEGO (my eyes glaze over), and always avoidable. When a secretary asks, "And what is your call in reference to?", I always answer with the one-word waker-upper, "Malfeasance."

Just as you should not modify a compound noun with a compound adjective (*one-word waker-upper* is hyphen-happy), you should not clutter up your prose with strings of little prepositions—unless you are reaching for biblical or poetical solemnity. (*Unless* is a way of slipping past *with the exception of.*)

When Lincoln wrote the preliminary Emancipation Proclamation in 1862, he invoked that solemnity with four prepositional phrases: "On the first day of January in the year of our Lord . . ." In a less portentous document, that device could put you to sleep.

Never double up on prepositions; better still, never double them. *Off of* is one too many; *I took a gold watch off of him* is the low language of thievery, but *I took a gold watch off him* sounds more high-class. Same with *of between* and *of from* in discussing ranges; kill the *of.*

The preposition string has best been satirized with the irate child's "What did you bring that book I didn't want to be read to out of up for?"

37

You should just avoid
confusing readers with
misplaced modifiers.

I could tell this guy was a loser when his press release came in. "The Republican candidate for Mayor, standing in front of a City apartment building in the South Bronx, disguised with decals of windows and flower pots . . ."

What was disguised with decals and pots—the candidate, the South Bronx or the building? This was not as egregious as the classic "Abraham Lincoln wrote the Gettysburg Address while traveling from Washington on the back of an envelope" but will do as a recent example of a modifying phrase placed in an ambiguous position.

In "Avoid confusing readers with misplaced modifiers," the fumbleruler suggests the object of avoidance should be "readers with misplaced modifiers" rather than writers who do the confusing. When I look at the logo of Batman, instead of seeing a menacing bat I keep seeing the reverse—a pair of tonsils. Same reversal with modifiers.

Sometimes you can fix the problem with a comma. The Hilton in Trinidad boasted: "The only hotel with tennis courts, a health club and TV in every room," which troubled guests who felt crowded by tennis courts in their rooms; the insertion of a comma after the health club would have let off some steam.

Put your prepositional modifier smack-dab against the word or phrase it qualifies. *A partridge is the object of song in a pear tree* does not have the

Yuletide charm of *A partridge in a pear tree is the object of song*.

With modifiers like *only, even, just, hardly, merely* and *nearly,* try to avoid placing the modifier in front of the verb. *I will even warn you* does not mean *I will warn even you.*

I would advise even you to be alert to double meanings: *Particulars of a government proposal are leaking out* should not read *Particulars are leaking out of a government proposal* unless that is true, in which case you have a better story.

38

*One will not have needed
the future perfect tense
in one's entire life.*

*T*ourist seeking a fish restaurant in Boston climbs in a taxicab and says to the cabbie, "Say, do you know where I can get scrod?" Cabbie replies admiringly: "Mister, I've been asked that a thousand times, but never before in the pluperfect subjunctive."

You want to know what *pluperfect* is. Literally, it's Latin for "more than perfect" (which would be "quite unique," also wrong), but using *perfect* in its early sense of "finished." In grammar, the *pluperfect,* or past perfect tense, uses *had* to locate an action completed before a time spoken of: *He had dined on scrod before he came to Boston.* Most people use the plain past tense, without the *had,* but what do most people know?

In the same way, the future perfect tense provides a specific depth of field in time to come: *I will have become tensed up about tenses by the time I finish my perfect martini.*

Damon Runyon, a writer who had been a sportswriter, introduced the *historical present* to the tense dodge: "When I hear Bugs Lonigan say this, I wish I am never born."

By the late 70s this had led (holdit—you have just experienced the *pluperfect*) to the *historical future.* In this weird modern verb form pioneered by sportscasters, a past event is described in a future tense.

"That will [*future tense*] bring up a third-down situation" calls a play that has already happened. "He swings and he misses—that'll be strike two," reports a past event in the future tense.

That's how tenses are born. When the sportscaster says, "If the runner had taken a longer lead, he would have had the base stolen cleanly," that *would have had* will be a great example of the cabdriver's *pluperfect subjunctive*.

39

*Place pronouns as close
as possible, especially in
long sentences—such as
those of ten or more words—
to their antecedents.*

*W*hen he was playing football for the New York Giants, Frank Gifford used to line up far from the rest of the team. His position became known as "the lonely end." Some pronouns identify with him.

Pronouns are verbal shorthand for those persons or things that you've mentioned before and don't want to load up your sentences by repeating. Handled properly, they deliver clarity as well as speed. (Hold on, now—what does *they* mean in that sentence? Pronouns? Persons? Things? I think I mean *pronouns,* but it's been so long that I forget. Recast.)

Pronouns, handled properly, deliver clarity as well as speed; they are verbal shorthand for persons and things you have already mentioned (or are very soon to mention) and you do not want to repeat. Ah, that feels better. The pronoun *they* is right up there near its antecedent, the noun *pronouns,* followed by the previously confusing *persons and things;* by thus splitting the zone defense, our no-longer-lonely end makes clear what noun it represents.

Always ask yourself, "Who's *who?*" I am reminded of the language maven, surrounded by grammar groupies (who oohed and ahhed at his syntax), who became insufferable. In that sentence, which *who* is doing what to whom? The *who* belonging to the maven is separated by the *who* belonging to the groupies, and separation is the enemy of the pronoun.

Recast. "I am reminded of the language maven

who became insufferable after being surrounded by grammar groupies oohing and ahhing at his syntax." (That is a sample sentence put in for illustrative purposes but is, unfortunately, unrelated to reality.)

Advice to the fuzzborn: Stop worrying about staying in touch with your feelings and stay in touch with your pronouns.

40

Eschew dialect, irregardless.

*Y*ou think you speak English? Get off it, man; what you speak is your *idiolect*—that amalgam of Standard English, local pronunciation, personal idiosyncrasy, and down-home regional dialect unique to you.

The question is: When do you observe the formality of Standard English and when do you let it all hang out?

I *dig* dialect; to be more current, I'm *into* dialect; to snap to Standard attention, I appreciate and select the occasion to use dialect. For that reason, I pepper my informal prose with *get off it, man* and such regional sexual allusions as *let it all hang out* (we're not talking about a shirttail, daddy-o).

Is it *airish* to insist on the pure language? *Airish,* from "puttin' on airs," is a Scotticism; our dialects offer variations from *stuck-up* and *high-falutin* to *high-hat* and *snooty.* The Standard English adjective for all these colorful words is *snobbish,* which is the best word to use if addressing a gathering of snobs.

That's the answer: Suit your language to your occasion and your audience. When chewing the fat with friends or shooting the breeze with colleagues, chew and shoot; when presenting a case to the Supreme Court, discuss the matter with decorum.

Here's the exception: (enough with the colons, already) Dialect may be used on a formal occasion when you and the audience know you are putting the informal phrase in quotes. *Enough with the colons, already* is a Yiddishism, like *not to worry* (which may be a Britishism); such regionalisms may be used to enliven formal discussion when done in a studied fashion.

Irregardless, for example, is *regardless* intentionally mixed up with *irrespective.* If you use it knowing it's a mistake, have fun; if you use it irregardless, it's a mistake.

41

Remember to never
split an infinitive.

*T*o split or not to split—or to not split? That is the question that divides the correction community.

The infinitive form in grammar, like the boundless sense of infinity elsewhere, is a verb unlimited by number, person or tense; to mark that unbounded form, the verb is preceded by *to*. The debate—as fierce as that over some theological principle—rages about whether sticking an adverb in the middle is a long step toward damnation.

Forget the fought-over principle; as Disraeli said, "Damn principles! Stick to your party." The party is about what you want the adverb to do.

Let's use the adverb *suddenly* to modify the infinitive *to split* and its object *the infinitive*.

If you want the adverb to modify the whole thought, put it up front: *suddenly to split the infinitive*.

If you want to emphasize your modification of the verb, stick it in the middle of the infinitive: *to suddenly split the infinitive*.

If you want to stress the effect on the object at the end, or just to add some punch at the end of your sentence, place the adverb at the end: *to split the infinitive suddenly.*

If you want to act the Latin pedant and bring down on yourself the hoots of native speakers, strain at not breaking the no-split rule: *to split suddenly the infinitive.*

"Every good literary craftsman splits his infinitives

when the sense demands it," wrote George Bernard Shaw. He shooed away the pedant who insisted on the inseparability of the verb and its pilot marker: "It is of no consequence whether he decides to go quickly or to quickly go."

Shaw should have added, "or quickly to go." He's not quite right: The placement of the adverb is subtly but definitely of consequence. *Quickly to go* accentuates the swiftness of the whole act of going; *to go quickly* and *to quickly go* stress the speedy way the business of going is done.

Got it? Now you can split.

42

Take the bull
by the hand
and don't mix
metaphors.

*W*hen figures of speech don't figure, we get unintentional humor.

The editorialist who soberly wrote that "the United States can fine-tune the end game," or the headline writer who chose "Slowdown Is Accelerating" or the government official who explained, "There is no quick lunch"—all were Mixmasters (or Cuisinartists) of metaphor.

What do you do when a senator announces that he and his committee have been "working like banshees"? You give him either a free lunch or a quick fix (not a mixture of both), explaining that one *works like a beaver* and *wails like a banshee;* a beaver puts in long hours at low pay building dams, while a banshee is an Irish-Scottish spirit known for the scary noise it makes in prophesying death.

Same kind of confusion with "fine-tune the end game": When a technological image like *fine-tune* (a compound verb that should be hyphenated) is combined with a chess trope like *end game* (a noun that does not need hyphenation), tuned-in grammarians feel checkmated and work themselves, beaver-like, into a banshee routine.

To avoid mixation, it helps to think about the meaning of your metaphor. Before writing, "My trial balloon went down the tubes," consider the origin of *down the tube* (singular). In surfing, the *tube* is a tunnel that forms in the face of a long wave just before the wave breaks; to shoot, or go down the tube, is one object of the sport, although the awkward position it requires led to the derogation *to tube it,* "to fail." At that point, non-surfers confused *down the tube* with *down the pipe* and *down the drain.* A seaside triumph became a bathroom disaster.

Beware of mixing *down the tube* with any unrelated metaphor; it's as tricky as *shooting the drain.*

43

Don't verb nouns.

*V*erbification—using a noun like *input* or *access* as a verb, or transforming *priority* into *prioritize*—is all the rage with bureaucratizers. (That's a new noun, back-formed from the verb *bureaucratize,* meaning "to make seem official," back-formed from the noun *bureaucrat.* I just made it up, to show how easy and silly this practice can be. Neither the noun-into-verb *bureaucratize* nor the ensuing verb-into-noun *bureaucratizer* is needed in the language; forget 'em. Also, don't stretch a parenthetical comment this far. And don't start sentences with *also* unless you're ostentatiously afterthinking.)

When a senator asked a Secretary of State, "Will you *burden-share?*" and the wary Secretary (Hi, Al) replied, "I'll have to *caveat* my response, Senator," verbification low-pointed.

We runwayed with *to host,* offtook with *to guest* and high-altitudinized with *to guest-host,* which means "to substitute for the regular host." All this is too-much-too-sooning.

No need to overboard ourselves on this: Functional shift (from one part of speech to another) is not new to English. My publisher at *The Times* has a thing about *contact* as a verb, and I'll have to get in touch with him about that because *contact* is an accepted improvement, the decision finalized by usage. Experience counts, and we've been using the noun *experience* as a verb for centuries.

Where do we draw the line? First, avoid confusion: *To gift* is bad, because the past participle, *gifted,* leaves it unclear whether the person is especially talented or corrupted by a payoff. Next, avoid lazy or unnecessary coinage: *Disincentivize* is no improvement over *discourage,* nor *disambiguate* over *clarify.*

Feel free, however, to use freshly minted verbs that fill a need: *Baby-sit* works, as do *intuit* and *position.* Don't lard your prose with the functional shifties, but don't bureaucratize about it, either.

44

De-accession euphemisms.

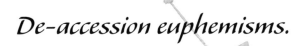

*T*he U.S. Embassy in Budapest used to hand each arriving diplomat a packet that included this warning: "It must be assumed that *available casual indigenous female companions* work for or cooperate with the Hungarian government security establishment." It would have been better for our counterintelligence efforts if somebody had said, "The local whores are spies."

In the same way, psychologists in the family-counseling way have been heard to question the efficacy of *intensive aversive intervention*. This was once called "spanking," or in Yiddish-speaking households, "a *potch* on the *tuchis*."

A *previously owned* Mercedes with low mileage is presumably a little-used car. A dealer in secondhand carpets advertised "*pre-loved* Orientals." And apple-juice manufacturers who add sweeteners to their products tartly eschew the word *sweetened* and have substituted *sophisticated*.

Welcome to the world of euphemism, where the national flower is a figleaf and the refusal to use painful words has not passed away.

Motive is central. Some euphemisms are simple kindness: Few could complain when the harsh *crippled* was replaced by *handicapped* and *disabled*, though *differently abled* is pushing it. Some are good taste: *Making love* is more appropriate in mixed company than *fornication* or its shorter synonyms. And some are creative: *Vomiting* is set aside on campus for the more imaginative *tossing your cookies* or *driving the big white porcelain bus.* The old euphemism for copulation—"sleeping together"—was improved by a later generation's "parallel parking."

But when the softening or prettifying panders to prudishness, or is motivated by commercial deception or bureaucratic obfuscation, the euphemism deserves termination with extreme prejudice. The language is being violated by an itsy-poo aversion to plain hard words. (I would have written *raped,* but *violated* seemed kinder and gentler.)

45

*Always pick on
the correct idiom.*

How are you?

There's an expression that thumbs its nose at grammatical analysis. *How do you feel?* is not much better, unless you mean "What method do you use to experience a tactile sensation?" The deep-structure crowd will have an answer to *howahya,* but on the surface, the phrase is grammatically meaningless.

We all know what it means—"What is the state of your health?" or "How well are you doing in whatever you do?"—because the phrase is an idiom. An idiom is a mistake that has been made so often for so long that any challenge to it is a mistake.

Some tidy types are driven to fill in the potholes on the road of language. If the ending *er* means "one who does" and the ending *ee* means "one to whom it is done," shouldn't an *escapee* who busts out of jail be an *escaper,* and shouldn't the prison guard left behind be the *escapee?* Such putative tidy-uppers are idiom savants.

Don't fight the problem; idioms is idioms. The trick is to get them right, and the victory is a triumph of ear over mind.

You can *hone down* a knife's edge, or an argument's point, and you can *home in on* an electronic beam leading to a destination, but you cannot *hone in on* anything.

Watch those idiomatic prepositions: You can follow *agree* with *to, with, on* or *about,* each with a different meaning, but never *from, of* or *than.* Follow *different* with *from,* and even get away with the less accepted *than,* but not *to,* except in Britain, where it's the other way around.

Idioms infuriate some people who insist on logic and revere order. Myself, I could care less.

46

If this were subjunctive,
I'm in the wrong mood.

*T*o pretend what ain't so is so, to suppose and hypothesize and play with possibilities, get in the mood the dreamers call "subjunctive." *Come what may,* this mood will shake off the shackles of fact and enshrine iffiness, *as it were.*

The purpose of this poet's mood is to state a condition contrary to fact. "Had we but world enough, and time," said the lover to his beloved holding out on him, "This coyness, lady, *were* no crime." "Ah," says the voice imitating Ronald Colman, "if I *were* king . . ." King is what he is not, which is why the verb is the conditional *were.*

So, the lazy reader is thinking, whenever I see an *if,* I'll use a *were.* That's a mistake, if ever there was one.

Let's say the Ronald Colman type, traveling incognito, really had been king; then he could say, "If I *was* king," and let them guess at what he knows to have been true. If you're examining a real likelihood, *if I was* is correct: "If I was speeding, your Honor, I didn't realize it."

Don't get stiffed by *if,* which does not always say it ain't so. Two paragraphs above, "if ever there *was* one" refers to the incontrovertible fact of a mistake, not a silly fiction. (Some mornings I get up looking like the Loch Ness Monster, if there *were* one.)

Most of the time, you're safe using the subjunctive *were* with the conditional *would.* (If I were sure of the lucidity of this explanation, I would scrap "most of the time.")

If the truth be known, *as it were* is a shortening of the subjunctive "as if it were true," and was originally used not to mean "so to speak" but to cast doubt on the preceding remark. Now you know all about the mysterious subjunctive, as it were.

47

Never, ever use
repetitive redundancies.

*R*epetition is reputation, the old flacks used to say, but anybody who gets a reputation for repetition these days is skewered by a band of Lexicographic Irregulars who lead a crusade against redundancy. They call their organization the Squad Squad.

"Fellow countrymen," begins a stump speaker, and the hooting begins: "You mean *fellow citizens* or plain *countrymen,* but you cannot correctly say something that means *fellow fellow men.*"

You cannot make a *new debut* or offer a *new innovation,* because the *new* is built into those words. I have been walloped for using a *large dollop,* because a *dollop* is a large scoop, and setting a *new record* because a *record* makes all "old records" *former records.* One elderly gentleman chastised me for writing *an old geezer* because, as he put it, "all us geezers are old."

When the Air Force came up with *attack bomber,* it spawned a generation of mod modifiers that has taken us to *garden salad,* but don't all bombers attack? Don't all salads come from gardens? Aren't all *pizzas* pies, all *gifts* free?

Some redundant phrases are so tightly fused that no grammarian dares put them asunder: *Never before* have I *joined together a bouquet of flowers* under *false pretenses.* These have broken the force of grammatical gravity to become idioms and can therefore thumb their noses at the Squad Squad.

But we can resist the trend toward *very unique,* and such mouth-filling tautologies that add nothing to meaning as *true facts* and *basic essentials,* which are circular in shape, colorless in color and stupid in nature.

48

"Avoid overuse of 'quotation "marks."'"

*A*mericans put the comma and the period inside quotation marks; the British put them outside. We use double marks to enclose the primary quotation and single marks to indicate quotations within quotations, while the British do precisely the opposite. That's because they're foreigners.

The verb is *quote;* the noun is *quotation,* but is being clipped to, and overtaken by, *quote:* The Twentieth Edition of Bartlett's will be *Bartlett's Quotes.* Do not feel unduly colloquial when saying, "He said, quotes:", rather than "He said, and I quote:", because that timesaver cannot be dislodged by rampart-dwellers.

However, draw the line against the overuse of the raised-eyebrow, get-this-whopper use of quotation marks to indicate a figurative rather than a literal sense of a word or phrase.

"The English teacher was 'appalled' at my approval of the clipping of some words." In that sentence, the word *appalled* is encased in marks not to indicate direct quotation, but to whisper, "What kind of easily shocked creep uses a word like *appalled?*"

The same device is used to cast doubt: "Preserve us from our 'evenhanded' friends." That uses quotation marks as a substitute for *so-called*, a term favored by Mischa Auer in *Ninotchka* and by Soviet diplomats in the pre-post-Cold War era: "America and her so-called democratic leadership, actually ruling circles." Native speakers rarely use *so-called,* preferring to inflect the suspect word, the sound of which we try to convey with quotation marks.

Sometimes it works: "The President 'misspoke himself'; actually, he confused himself and us." Often, it comes across as heavyhanded sarcasm: "With typical 'openness,' the Russian 'spokesman' (we all know he's a former KGB colonel) offered his version of 'truth,' Moscow-style. . . ."

No need to scrap irony; just lay off the eye-rolling punctuation unless you suspect that your reader is unlikely to get your point. In that case, elevate them sights a little lower, with a phrase like *in what they call* or *said to be*.

49

*Never use prepositions
to end sentences with.*

*F*orget Winston Churchill's denunciation of a copy editor who dared to apply this rule to his immortal prose: "This is the type of arrant pedantry up with which I will not put!" The copy editor was right in resisting the "with" at the end of a sentence. Churchill was shrewd enough to use his own fumblerule to show how attempts to avoid ending sentences with prepositions could be labored and ludicrous, but "This is an impertinence I will not put up with" is better expressed as "I will not put up with this impertinence."

"She was the girl I always dreamed of" comes more comfortably to the tongue, despite its closing preposition, than "She was the girl about whom I always dreamed," the sort of sentence in which not even the most rigid grammarians find pleasure. Back up to look at that last sentence, and try: "The sort of sentence not even the most rigid grammarians find pleasure in." No, the first way was better, because it ends crisply with the noun "pleasure," but I'll grant it does contain that stiff *in which*. Better than both would be "Not even the most rigid grammarian would find pleasure in that sort of sentence." When you find yourself in a preposition-ending pickle, be like a Broadway producer with a recalcitrant star: Recast.

Weigh the inelegance of a final preposition against the stiffness of a formulation that knocks itself out avoiding such inelegance. Sometimes invincible idiom dictates the preposition ("That's what lit-tle girls are made of"); in that case, relax and enjoy it. Other times, awkwardness can be avoided with a quick fix: "Bankruptcy, my dear fellow, is what we're looking at" can be switched to "We're looking at bankruptcy, you idiot."

Rigidity is out; flexibility is in. But don't be so flexible as to feel yourself forced by hang-loose language slobs always to leave "in" in.

50

Last but not least, avoid clichés like the plague.

*O*ld-timers can remember when all *denials* were *flat.* Then times changed, and *flat* fell flat, giving way to *flat-out,* a locution taken from the pressing of the accelerator against the car floor in auto racing (source of *put the pedal to the metal*). Nowadays White House spokespersons issue *flat-out denials* about policy changes, insisting only that the President "misspoke."

What became of the plain, unadorned adjective *flat,* divorced from its long wedding to *denial?* It found a home in sports clichés, as the universally favored description of a team that just cannot work up any enthusiasm: "The Cowboys are *flat* today, but the Bears really *came to play.*"

A cliché is a turn of phrase that is, not to coin a phrase, *plumb tuckered out.* (Whenever you see *to coin a phrase* or *as they say,* prepare for a cliché; the writer is too self-conscious to use a trite expression without apology.) The French word means "stereotype," a printing plate, and comes from the German *Klitsch,* a lump of clay that becomes a mold.

"And after God made our dear departed friend," the eulogist says, "He *broke the mold.*" That's Mr. Cliché, and we *shall not look upon his like again* (which was a fresh phrase only four centuries ago, when Shakespeare's Hamlet used it about his father). Like brief-forms in shorthand, save-gets in computer programming or prefabricated modules in homebuilding, clichés are evidence of thought-free writing.

Not every tried-and-true expression is a cliché—
tried and true is robust if well used—and the use of
familiar terms like *Nosy Parker* or *traffic snarl* enlivens
our prose. But cock an ear to this recent memo from
the copy chief of *Time* magazine, fumbleruling his
troops: "Hold your feet to the fire, keep your nose
to the grindstone and go through your copy with a
fine-toothed comb."

Recognitions and Thanks

*T*his is what is customarily known as the Acknowledgments page. The rubbery verb *acknowledge* has meanings that range from "notice and respond" to the legal "certify" to the grudging "admit to be true."

As a plural noun, *acknowledgments* carries a scholarly connotation of "my conscience forces me to this"; it's a mean-spirited meaning, offering only a cool and condescending nod to those who deserve more.

Why do we literary types go along with words that don't convey what we mean? Convention is the reason. The movie people have a better word: *credits*. (Unfortunately, the credits are said to "crawl" up the screen, which demeans them a bit.)

With neither shame nor patronization, I recognize the help given me by Ann Elise Rubin and Jeffrey McQuain, my editorial assistants at *The New York Times*, and to Nancy Evans and Sally Arteseros, my editors at Doubleday, as well as the copy editor, Chaucy Bennetts. This edition's editors are Amy Cherry and Lucinda Bartley, the designer is Margaret M. Wagner, and the copy editor is Sarah England. I am also indebted to (*last but not least, avoid clichés like the plague*)—I also want to thank the corps of language lovers called the Lexicographic Irregulars, including the Gotcha! Gang, the Nitpickers' League and the Nitpicker's League, for the constant haranguing-by-mail that enriches my column, ennobles my undertakings and enlivens my life.